A Resting Place

Gilbert McInnis

A Resting Place

Gilbert McInnis

InExile Publications
Quebec

National Library of Canada Cataloguing in Publication
McInnis, Gilbert (1963-)

A Resting Place / Gilbert McInnis

ISBN: 978-0-9876759-3-4

Canadian Poetry, Poetry, Nature

.

Printed in Canada for InExile Publications
Typesetting & Cover Design: InExile Design

LIST OF POEMS

DEDICATION

I dedicate this book to my children: Joshua, Mélodie, Maggie, and Joseph. If you ever wondered where your father was at times, he was seeking out a place to rest and to feel inspired to write these poems. When I am absent, you can read these poems, for in reading them, you will discover more about me and about you.

ACKNOWLEDGMENT

I am very grateful for Dr. Mrinal Kanti-Ray's insightful comments in the preparation of these poems for publication.

Trees Outside My Window

I look across my
yard to see the same tree,
as many trees.
And with every season
you bring to me
similar thoughts, but
in different colours,
as would different trees.

In the spring, I witness buds
being born, then
blossom to oily green.
With every fall of rain,
you paint them by numbers
into my memories,
leaving me to think of what
I have to do.

On those heated nights
of patio whispers — I look over
to you, body tight and young,
making memories that will carry
me into the fall.

When I see the first sacrificial colour
spring from your roots, it grows

into orange, then to yellow, leaving
green to margins and then
melting away.

Into a minority separating me
from you tree until that crisp morning,
when you'll paint your pigments onto
my canvas of thoughts,
where they'll bleed away into white,
leaving me to think of spring again,
how you'll be born once more.
Because, "Your head so much concerned
with outer, Mine with inner, weather."

Rivers that run dry

Rivers that run dry
are often on my mind.
They hide in lusty forests,
and are often not heard.
Even in the quietest moments
of your concrete sea — you won't
hear them, but they exist.
I am a witness to them.

I've sought them out in those
hidden places, places where
I can't be heard.
Even large forging rivers
in springtime run without
your audience, but I carry
them to you. I am a bringer
of dry rivers.

The birds give audience to them,
and keep them company,
at night-time and in silence.
They flow peacefully together,
singing of dry rivers,
when I send them to you.

A warm breeze carries them.
They bring that familiar fragrance

that carries dry rivers to you.
In the stillness of my time,
I feel them roaring within,
roaring with my soul to tell you.

There will be a time when
that roaring will flow into
peaceful thoughts.

Touch the river, taste it,
let it flow around your body.
Let it baptize you.
Plunge yourself into its darkness,
its secrecy, its fear.

And when you swim
in that fear, it will become
your friend — a river friend.
I carry friends to you.

And when you hear
the songs of the rivers,
or when they greet you,
they will then run dry.

Dry rivers bring no fear.
Dry rivers bring friends
by melodies, by smells,
by echoes — echoes of my friends. ·

The sounds you hear,
I send them to you.
I am a bringer of rivers that run dry.

Light and Shadow

Light and shadow,
black and white,
grey is the colour,
when all come together.

Your eye is the seam,
the notes on a page.
Your heart is the beat
that drives this song.

Can't you see, can't you feel
when I write you in these colours?

The leaves in the trees
bleed into me,
green as the spring,
yellow as the fall.

The wind will take them,
they'll lie in the snow,
as notes on the page
come to an end.

Can't you see, can't you feel
when I write you in these colours?

Heart Beats More Than Love

Look into my eyes
and you may see
a world of desire,
or in these eyes
a light that burns
more than fire.

Will you give a moment
or at least lend me
your precious time?
I hope I'm worth
everything they tell you
and more…because
a heart beats more than blood,
a soul needs more than love.

And now is the time
for you to contemplate
your secret escape,
and to make a move
into your sacred silence.

Will you give me a moment?
Look into my eyes
that burn more than fire.
I hope I'm worth
your secret escape
or a sacred silence…because

my heart bleeds more than blood,
my soul needs more than love,
my heart beats for your love,
my soul bleeds in your blood.

Copper Rock

Out on Copper Rock
I lie warm, waiting,
on the edge of its surface with my feet
immersed in the bubbling
current fleeting by.

I witness an arcing
against the tree tops
on the opposite bank.
The atomic blanket caresses
each olive-coloured sheet,
as nature passes over it
on its way, moving each one
from warmth to memories of warmth,
then to shadows.

The water slackens its rhythm
around my feet, and I hear it drift from
bubbling and chugging
to lapping tranquillity.

I wonder at the canvas
of eternal change above.
Idly, a white castle is transformed into
a silver lined foetus, with one omniscient Eye
appearing from the whiteness.
With nodal exactness, it

examines me lying there
on the bronze surface.
It proceeds through me, as an x-ray
would, to locate my bones.

Somewhere within me, it finds a fracture.
I close my eyes, and it rests there.
It's aware of me, aware of it.
I grow colder.
Perhaps the Eye has closed.

It searches out my thoughts,
and when they come,
I remember a warm feeling,
a pleasing feeling caressing me
as it passed on its way.
And when I open my eyes,
the shadow is on me!

The bells have finished ringing

The bells have finished ringing,
but the echoes remain to entertain
the valley of distant people.
They hear the chimes — those ancient
vibrations — ringing, pulsing, orgasmic
sounds of the body being crucified.

Blood purging from its pores,
while the bells motion to and fro,
rocking on a steel bar.
The bellman's hands slide
up and down the rope,
bringing the metallic flesh
to a bang.

A hammer head thrust itself
against the surface, hurling
each part of the melody
into a void of darkness.

A train is heard off in the distance
while hammers bang out their notes,
thrashing against the ironclad, tossing the bell's fruit
into the humid air overlying the community.

Where a metal machine plunges along its path,
forcing itself through the gardens of Springfield,
its engine drives the wind mad,

piercing the apathetic air and whipping
out its white disgust.
Whipping out its compulsion, slapping sounds of metal on
metal-ringing, pulsing, ejaculating the white traces of
memories across the sky in harmonies, which are dispersed
lightly by the wind.

A Resting Place

I lie against a smooth rock
shaded by a towering oak tree.
Not too far from a lonely stream, I can see a sun beam,
swimming on the bubbling blue water,
disappearing under young dipping leaves down a ways,
where perhaps I hear a young thin girl.
Or it could be the wiper-willow
calling out in the dense forest.
Overhead a metallic ringing echo
passes emerald tops,
as the wind would over a rye field in autumn.
I hear them calling me,
calling me while I inhale
a fusion of wild raspberries,
mixed with hidden sweet grass.
Again, I hear the bells, but for now
I will stay in my resting place, and listen to the melodic
stream creating a symphony in my head,
to the rhythmic backdrop of percussive grasshoppers
chattering tick, tick, tick.

Immaterial Pain

Look in my eyes
through the disguise
into the nexus of my soul.
You will feel my pain.
Of long awaited desire
to write lines that never begin, never end.

The pain that gives life —
life to a story, a human story
that starts in pain and journeys
without clear answers
to an immaterial end.

Can you see beyond that story of yours?
If you do, does it cause you pain?
Perhaps we should then materialize ourselves
to steel bodies that give no pain away,
if they are really cold bodies.
Cold bodies that are formed by elements
pumped into it, and when activated
to the temperature of desire,
less two degrees, changes
according to its environment.
Conditioned properly, and with a method,
a painful method, because it is material.

Nuclear Effects

My brain is an apocalyptic dilemma
shooting protons into society,
separating philosophical atoms and
leaving radiant thoughts behind.
A nuclear dilemma that
mushrooms in emotions.
My head feels like a rocket, erect and throbbing.
Explosion!
The protons spray out,
each transporting their light into the darkness.

First chain reaction: we call ourselves artists
who stand in front of coloured designs
that a computer sexes onto a glossy sheet.
We are choking art to death!

Second chain reaction: she gives birth alone
to statutes created in a factory.
Each one mixed in a laboratory,
then transferred to a heating machine
where it incubates and awaits
a cooling time on the assembly line.
Millions of them running down the conveyor belt.
Glossy porcelain dolls side by side, male and female.
I can see them bouncing up and down
as they move towards their cardboard destiny.

Third chain reaction: T.V. or T.B.
Electronic theatre where living rooms
are molded into one direction worshipping silicone.
I won't worship mine until it has a better attitude.

When red lips touch a page

I stare and I stare
at the lines on the page.
They read: "I love you,"
but I can't find a name.
The stars in the skies
might show me your eyes.
They look so much alike
when I first saw them that night.
I don't know who you are,
I can't make out a face.
All I can see is red lips signed to a page.

I stare and I stare
at lines drawn by those lips
untill I can read what they say:
"draw an image of my face."
I search out a pair stars
to play the part of your eyes.
Then I toss up those red lips
to fill that empty space.
Now I know who you are.
Now I can make out your face.
From what I can see,
when red lips touch a page,
when red lips kiss a face.

A Million Doors

I was conceived in a house of a million doors
to journey through a labyrinth, closing then opening,
where inside of one door I see a man
sitting constipating, contemplating, then rationalizing his
past to the future.
And in another door, a woman hurries about
making appointments so she can rest her feet
at the end of her day to look forward to tomorrow's door.
At another door, I take the handle firmly,
but I hesitate...droplets of emotional sweat
flowing out together from my flesh like a receding tide,
taking earth out into the sea.

I opened the door and revel in disgust at the darkness —
"The horror, the horror."
It molded around my flesh, but did not pierce my pores
through to the stream of my blood.
Two currents don't run well side by side.
One thinking the other wrong by today's measures
which the other considering wrong by the cross.
Only if we had read Kurtz's 17 pages,
then we'd know the *intended*.
As Marlow, we've turned our backs on her too.
Jesus once said, "If they don't listen to the prophets,
they won't listen to the resurrected."

Closing that door, I fled to another where inside
was a circular room with chairs around the parameter.

Each chair had to have another beside it; it's natural.
Every woman sat alone waiting, and I worked my way
around the room stopping at the first.
When I finished with one *intended,*
I moved onto another.
I sat with the second looking for answers to life
more desperate now. But I received none.
I continued onto the next, then the next ...
Each chair was a new place
and a rebirth for me — a born again.

I came round to the door,
I entered to discover this —
a circular room goes nowhere just in circles.
As I exited, another man was entering,
and I tried to warn him of the impending cyclic-peril.
He replied: "All my life's a circle, sunrise to sundown,
moon rolls through the night-time
until the daybreak comes around."
Then I saw him take his place on a warm chair.
He went from chair to chair,
and I left knowing his sudden return.

I entered into another room where a baby
sat in the middle of the floor playing with small blocks.
A woman passed by the baby and exited through a door
on the opposite side.

Another woman with a brief case entered the room,
then stopped beside the baby, looked at her watch,

then followed the other woman through the door.
At last came a man into the room
and walked to the child.
He was interrupted by the ringing of his cellular phone.

He talked as he walked and then went off towards the door
where the first woman had left by.
So they left me and the child all alone to play.
I sat down on my knees and hands, gazing at him,
then the child disappeared through my legs.
And when I stood up, I was the only person in the room!

I'd like to knock on your door

How sweet your presence I felt
when I heard your brown skin knock on my heart.
And when I opened the door, your door,
I smelt the fruit of wine,
wine between two, not one.
Then I heard the sound of a slide guitar
falling on lonely heartstrings.

It drew me, drew me, like a straight line,
to you, to cuddle, to caress,
then moved me with nature's fall into the grass,
into those thin lip-like leaves that heal,
even for knuckles that have knocked all night
for an awaken lover who has fallen asleep.
In those brown fingers wrapped around
by green grass leaves until they've dissolved
and become one in red wine.

When I hear music

When I hear music, you are there.
When I read a book, your face is
written all over its characters.
I would not say to myself "I love her."
I rather wait in silence
until my soul told me stories.

And when you drift off to sleep
thousands of moments away,
you ask me in your healing heart
to speak to you in songs and tales
of ancient heroes that make
up our days.

As you slide away from your pain
into a slippery slope, downward
on the lip of that smile,
I am kept from seeing or touching,
left alone from any part of you.

You spread yourself across a place
ingenuously, an open door
that I've heard knocked on by
numerous lovers while I waited
alone in my room.

You lay on that bed while I seek out
the Valkyries to take you away.

My heart grows weak
as you fade into unconsciousness,
for they refuse your pleadings.

I will take you to where
the wounded find peace
in my arms of flowing blood
into the river of loneliness,
which moves down your body
between your legs, awakening
a long lost feeling inside of me.
Wake up, wake up. Please wake up!!!

To smell the salt air

To smell the salt air as I return closer
to the sea, that circular air.
And to wash my feet in those washing waves
is to fix my soul to the souls of maritime.
I return as I will again, and again.
To hear those watery rhythms being plucked from
the metal strings of a flat-top,
from within the Hitching Post,
where melodies carry out horse windows
to the ears of companions sitting around a fire,
listening to the sounds made by the wood in the fire
of human endeavours.

Turn over another log, turn over another ditty,
turn over another memory.
Forge them so they will go up like smoke to the sky,
blown around in our deeper consciousness,
by that circular wind carrying these remnants forever,
forever around, and over, and over again.
Where at a distance, when the smoke can be seen, or
sounds heard, it signifies a place, where people are
gathering to make memories and melodies.
Listen to them, played on wood or by wood,
to returning friends, to each other's memories,
and coming out to consciousness.
So we can hear just one more song.

Cape Split

I felt the spirit out on the sea
coming off the Atlantic,
all the way down from Digby,

> caressing her neck
> as the waves may do
> moving into the cove.

The waves rise up,
the waves fall down
untill it makes its way
every day to the Split.

Two times a day
the rivers of the world
flow to the Fundy
untill the spirit takes it away,
takes it away,

> caressing her neck
> as the waves may do
> moving into the cove.

The waves rise up,
the waves fall down
untill it makes its way
every day to the Split.

If you run down her spine
for an hour or two,
you can feel the roar
of her whirlpool,
as she takes you in,
takes you in,

        caressing her neck
     as the waves may do
     moving into the cove.

The waves rise up,
the waves fall down
untill it makes its way
every day to the Split.

Up high on the cliff,
the mother falcon soars
to the cries of her babes,
as the sun sets on the shore,

        caressing her neck
     as the waves may do
     moving into the cove.

The waves rise up,
the waves fall down
untill it makes its way
every day to the Split.

Flesh leaps out

What happens
when flesh enters the eyes,
eyes that crucify Christ?
Blink! and sin is locked in.

My body becomes a prison
and my heart a cell.
I serve darkness
untill my eyes open.

Free to light, but according
to science, made of colours.
I can't see
colours in a rainbow.

Baptized in a rain of
unseen particles jumping
across the universe
to my cell window.
When I open my eyes,
flesh leaps out!

Away

When I woke up alone today,
I found out the moon was drifting away.
Then I thought about you the other night,
with that rose against your lips
in the moon light.
If the moon's moving, it's moving me.
The moon's moving me away.
Away.

That night I looked into your eyes,
I saw the moon in the heavenly skies.
And when you left me alone that night,
I saw the moon drifting away in the light.
If the moon's moving, it's moving me.
The moon's moving me away.
Away.

As the moon changes our tide,
your absence touches me inside.
And what do you want me to do?
And what do you want me to say?
If the moon's moving, it's moving me.
The moon's moving me away.
Away.

I reduce my imagination

I reduce my imagination
to chemicals spotted out onto a page
in order to create an image of a flowing
river in your mind.

Must I reduce my pain to only lines?
Are apes aware of poetry?
Do you really believe genes
inspire poetic incantations?

But what about those summer nights
that stuck our misgivings together,
when our orbs met on a determined path,
face to face, to the backdrop of trillions of spectators
twinkling an eye, who was I?

Is my love derived from a 4½ second
muscle contraction?
(About the same length of time it took you to read this).

What about candles spraying images
against the walls like music all over our souls,
the thrill, the expectation, the great expectation,
that great preparation which comes in time:
there is a time to plant,
a time to love, a time to hate,
and a time to relate.

And when you are alone,
is it the thought of my genes that will comfort you?
Hold you, look at you, caress you,
or listen to you while you speak.
And when I am dead and gone,
will you still remember me
or will it be the memory of my DNA
that will turn you to me?

Or will you hear the melodies
breathed into your soul
behind those closed doors?
Will you think about them as mathematical incantations
which heightened your love?

Remember, I plucked them out on metal strings
with a plastic pick, while reflecting on your smile.
You'll remember me when those songs have ended,
after the vibrations of 440 per something have stopped.

The Eye of the Universe

The sun is overhead
and I lie on this bench,
looking into the eye of the universe.
I look up while it is pierced through
by lovely green leaves.

These are moments
when the wind shakes the branches back and forth,
and rays shine through, hotter and more brilliant,
then with shade into the cool.
And I hear melodies that carry me away
as each warm ray passes through me.

I follow it through portholes of greenery
descending, a beam narrow and straight.
This light falls upon my shoulder
while a sensation moves through me.
What do I see on the ground?
Is it the sun or a pattern of shades — shaded black?
I watch these patterns move about.
They shift here and there, but not moving far.
A strong wind would move them further.

These patterns will dissipate
at the end of autumn or in the winter,
leaving shadows of naked branches
to be projected upon the ground.

David and Bathsheba in my heart

David and Bathsheba in my heart
return in those lonely moments of the day.
When the warm liquid of my body
is their body, my home.
Even the arching flames of the
universal Sun would visit
each seed and bring them to
fruition, until a crack in the shell
would appear, birthing it into the
seam of my life.

A green head surges up
from the earthly womb
and erects to the universal eye,
throbbing until it is married
to a womb-like leaf,
formed by a Barbie doll.

And David and Bathsheba in my heart
returned to multiply them,
into future conceptions,
until coloured leaves fall on the ground
and be covered by a white blanket of cold.

Taj Mahal May Close

20, 000 men and twenty years,
over one departed loving friend,
of one bereaved man.

His grief echoed out in each hammered stone
and polished into white marble,
where he will gaze upon her face
as each setting sun casts a rosy hue over it.

"All for one woman," voices echoed about,
in octavated sounds, passing through
portals and coming together in one.

Where old women's eyes pierced through a
marble screen, squinting at foreign script,
and demanding explanations, while their men
gazed all around them at the remnants
of 20, 000 men, whom for twenty years,
gave birth to her final womb.

Fragrant Autumn

The trees are all bare now,
and the apples have fallen to the ground.
While footsteps hurry away,
I inhale the fragrance of autumn.

The wind carries freshly cut wood my way,
then I see it far off lying in the sun.
These golden walls implode images of sacred homes,
and they explode fires in me.

Pipe tobacco carries
remnants of fatherly images,
as it hovers across a stream,
where it mingles with a misty breeze.

I follow it through yellow leaves
where humans and transforming machines
crush freshly fallen apples in a wooden womb,
sending up sprays to make autumn perfume.

A Walk to Wood Ends

You took me on a walk
that autumn day,
along a path with paint
Some red, some yellow,
some orange and some green.
Along the way, you talked about
the family's houses,
some empty and some filled
in summer days.

We walked by a little path
that led down to a pool.
You said it was about twenty feet deep —
a big pool, or things like that, as I remember.
You went on and on while your voice fused
with bird sounds overhead.

We wondered awhile
about an empty space, marked out
by the grass and two trees wanting life,
a life you remembered as a child.
You said a house used to be there,
but had burnt to the ground,
leaving the two in the front-yard
as witnesses to what occurred.

At the top of a hill
you showed me a toboggan run,

taken over by small trees.
It ended near to the river bank,
which I thought dangerous
for a child, but for you, only fun.

You took me by the hand
to a spot in a field, where in two places
wood pieces were shattered.
You told me how you used to chop for fun.
And I looked at your memories
lying there, piecing them together in my mind.

"The pond is near. Shall we go?"
I followed you to a hedge,
a familiar place in my memory.
It was round, deep in the center.
The colour of fall is on the far side.

Blowing across this side were leaves,
some red, some yellow, some orange
and some green, reminders, reminding us
of our first fall.

You shared how in winter
your dad would clear away a spot,
just for you to skate.
Then you invited me to come
at Christmas to clear another.
We would then sit around the fire
and drink drinks, nice and warm.

"The pond's deep and good for swimming."
"It was always fun here."
I mused upon spring,
and how lonely the pond must be.

We continued along the path
where I spotted at the top of a hill
a cemetery gate.
On the iron gate was writ "Wood Ends."
I opened it and we went in for a pleasant visit.
There I saw the river below,
the paint by number trees,
the other places we had visited,
and the pond too.

We walked down and down.
You talked about your father.
Beside a glossy headstone, I stopped ...
I listened to the wind dry up leaves overhead,
leaves that would shortly fall to the ground.
Written on the stone side was
Vigor, Virtus, Viritae,
meaning 'Vigor, Virtue and Truth.'
  "So he was a man of strength."
"Yes."
"Who is he? Did you know him?"
"Oh, he is my father!"
"It's a nice place to visit."
"Sure!"

We departed, leaving through the gate.
All I recall now is sitting with you
in a whickered chair.
I handed you a poem "Fall" to read.
Then we talked and talked.
And I fell and fell …

Fall

Fall into winter
when the coloured leaves remind you
of a never-ending end.

Red is the colour of blood,
and blood is the sacrificial flow for life.
Yellow reminds us of the coward's fear,
the fear of the unknown.
Orange brings us a perfume
when squeezed from a peel.

A mist off the river in the morn,
beyond the church steeple,
stirs up coloured images
that leave as soon as the ivory blanket
covers them.

Fall slumbers into
a rainbow of memories,
painted across a river's surface.

Crickets sing into a chorus of change,
then peter into other melodies.
The whispers of a summer night
are loaded into our minds.
Coloured whispers of red, yellow, and orange
take over, leaving green to the fringe —
a green driven by fears and sacrifices.

I smell your smell as the virgin morning.
I peel off your green and red dress.
I squeeze your fruit into my mouth,
and the juice permeates my senses,
recalling me to the images of red, yellow,
and orange.

Our House?

I saw an old wooden house
deserted in a field leaning to the right.
A strong wind coming from the left is to blame?
The roof had a bow and the
rain poured hard on it.

Once children ran about there,
upon new pine boards
on their way to the field.
The y played hide-and-seek
in the golden wheat their father planted.
A woman was cooking on a stove
while her husband was reading a paper.

Now the house is inhabited by the wind
finding its way through each bedroom
looking for someone to play.

Apples in a Tree

I see apples in a tree,
and snow at its feet.
Branches, black, stretching
open to the field,
partly covered in snow.
Plenty of windfalls,
some hidden and some between the grass.

Why have the pickers left overripe fruit,
all alone and hanging still?
Christmas ornaments,
green, red, yellow,
as if in bed at night.

Havin' spoken to the pickers,
with a voice inaudible,
nature bids us,
come pick my ready fruit before it falls.

Autumn Night Sky

In an autumn night sky,
I saw pulsating emerald spirits
dance across the milky spray
towards a scene visible
on the handle of the big dipper.
Visible there was also a party
held in honour of the Great Northern Light
who sat upon a throne at the tip,
while eyeing nuclear footsteps explode.
The dancing steps looked like
fluctuating atomic forms.
On the horizon broke out the radiant dawn
that put a stop to this memory.

Gilbert McInnis

The Spider Within

What is it in a spider
hanging from its own string,
pane of glass on one side
and on the other screen?
It may move up a distance,
and it may slide down.
But movement beyond
the glass is impossible,
unless some human lift the window
and give it more to go beyond.

But on the other side
is the screen–with perforated
holes–letting in fresh air
and life from the outside.
Yet small holes, enough, to keep it within.
And when the winter air comes,
and then the snow,
that same fresh air from summer
will turn cold and freeze it's organs.

But for now, it may move up,
a little, and it may slide
down.

44

The Bare Trees

A violent wind has blown away the colours.
Soon soft snow will lie upon the limbs
and the temperature will fall.
The rain descends.
Bare branches fight back
making whipping sounds at night.
Bare branches — skeletal branches,
waiting eagerly for spring to come,
to regenerate from buds.

But until that date,
they will notice life about and around.
Perhaps a small boy, stocky and short
will carry a stick onto a ice surface,
where underneath he spies a universe of bubbles
captured by time, frozen and unnoticed.

Snowfall

Rising up from the womb of time
does the snow sail downwards,
bouncing round and round
in all directions.
Then landing on shoulders
passing down side-streets,
or seen on the branches of the trees,
or empty wooden houses.

The wind forms bed and blanket for the snow,
so no need for heated home or fire place.
Within it is contained the invisible germs
which sprout into flakes
despite the life-chilling wind.

Each form into an array of fleshly designs,
chartering a coarse day after day in us
the feeling of a virgin fall.
We have fallen with them, time and time again.

We who fall with them forget their fall soon after,
so life is relived after each fall still,
and is known by others in a community
of unexpected whiteness.

Passing Life

There is something about your
plush chestnut coloured strands
blowing in the autumn wind,
mingling with scattered flakes
hopelessly riding on the waves
until they lie on your warm neck.

A man with a torn and unclean scarf,
and grizzled face stares
as you pass him by.
His thoughts stop momentarily
as your image can been seen
on the surface of his eyes.

He is now caught in a dilemma.
He clenches a cigarette between
his brown stained fingers.
He is a passive protagonist
faced with an active antagonist
moving around him and quickly onto other stories
while leaving him behind to contemplate his-story.

You stop and look at a window display.
He admires you by the reflection in the glass.
When you depart he even imagines your face
still stuck there on the glass, until the remnant
can no longer feed his mind.

But he is left with an image that remains in his mind
until he is awakened at night to primordial groaning
which purged it into the darkness.
His eyes open to image on the flat glass.

Passing Snow

A floating white sea comes
and sets a blanketed ground.
A covert wind warned me of your visit.
So relax, come, slowly and gently,
and lay down and add your white
cover to an ever green tree,
where underneath I see a small deer,
chewing her last, then leaving small
dots..... .. ..in the surface.

But not so tiny as the mouse next to a house,
sinking into crevasses along its journey.
Over head a black raven stares,
while flapping white powder down.
It turns to a trickle, flowing down my flesh
into the hollow of my spine — shiver!

Underneath my feet I hear the sounds
of crunching crisp water and it brings
back a miracle to my thoughts.

Slowly, through my eyes, an image enters;
a blaze off in the distance lowers itself
to rest upon the earth,
stretching its brilliant wings across
the land while exploding white
and golden waves into sparkles.

Gilbert McInnis

When I look behind me a white blanket moves
over the land on a journey, passing naked trees,
erecting itself on roof tops, breasty hillsides,
and on top of roads, until it ends in my face.

I don't know where it came from,
and I surely don't know where it is going.
But I know one thing for certain,
as long as winter is, it goes where it wants.

A Stream of Snow

A stream of city lights,
waves across the bay.
Images making patterns,
searching out to play.
Moonlight spray on the land
heralds in the dew,
while a walker on a shoreline
journeys between the two.
Do you see her there
inside a stream of snow?
An image on a web,
stripped and no place to go.
Screaming sirens are here,
the night takes its turn.
As a wave splashes its way
into our hearts, it burns.
I sense a rush of fire,
would you free my soul?
Into an image in time,
rescue me, it's too cold.
Do you see us there
inside a stream of snow?
An image on a web
stripped and no place to go.

Gilbert McInnis

I saw a universe hanging onto a tree

I saw a universe hanging onto a tree
under a full moon last night.
Just like any other universe,
there were stars pulsating time away.
Some of them iced to a branch
while the wind passed over them.

It made its way around the
form of the branches, shaking each one,
sometimes violently, then the full moon
casts a light onto them.

Within this outer form of the tree,
a cloud of ice-dust floated relatively about,
sometimes twinkling off light.
Then each crystal, within, turned by the wind
to face the moon.
In this moment of galactic arcing,
they fused to my soul.

Look in now, and there you will see
this universe floating upon the
wet surface of my eyes.

The Age of Icicles

This is the age of icicles
when in the morning you can
find them still frosty from the night.
Firm enough that little boys
can pick them from Dery House,
like apples from a tree,
the tree placed in the Garden.
They may suck on them, perhaps
some sticking to their tongues, until
the warmth comes and releases them.
Then, they drip and drip water to
the ground, baptizing the spring earth below.

Warmer weather brings more drops,
rhythmically dropping to the ground,
while a chorus of birds sing
their morning chant to the river surging by.

In the high noon of defeat,
the icicles are crucified,
with each atomic light.
They fall to the surface
and sound off like shattered pottery
breaking over Shoal's dirt floor,
waiting there to be baptized by the
drops that drip and drip and drip...

ABOUT THE AUTHOR

Gilbert McInnis has earned his Ph.D in English Literature at Université Laval. He recently published a monograph, *Evolutionary Mythology in the Writings of Kurt Vonnegut* (2011). He is the founder of *InExile* Publications, which has re-published Paul Goodman's *Moral Ambiguity of America*, a debut work by the American poet Erik Wackernagel's *She Bang Slam* and Sir Leonard Woolley's *Ur of Chaldees*. He taught English literature at Université Laval, Université Chicoutimi and Bishop's University in Québec, at Grenfell College in Newfoundland, and at Acadia University in Nova Scotia.